LEARNING HTML II

BY

ALIYU MUHAMMAD

DEDICATION

To the humble courage great ones among us who exemplify how leadership
is a choice not a position.

CONTENTS

ABOUT THE BOOK

LEARNING HTML II .Is an indispensable guide for anyone looking to delve into the captivating world of HTML and unleash their creativity on the web. Whether you're a novice or an experienced developer this comprehensive book will equip you with knowledge and skills needed to harness the full potential of HTML.

INTRODUCTION TO HTML

HTML is a **markup** language for **describing** web documents (web pages)

- HTML stands for **Hyper Text Markup Language**
- A markup language is a set of **markup tags**
- HTML documents are described by **HTML tags**
- Each HTML tag **describes** different document content

HTML is the backbone of every web page, proving the structure and content that browsers use to display information.

HTML uses a set of tags to define the structure and element of a webpage. These tags are enclosed in angle brackets < > and are composed of an opening opening tag and a closing tag. The content between the tags represents the data or information that is displayed on the web page

Here is an Open tag and closed tag

Open tag < >

Closed tag </>

What you can do with HTML

With HTML you can create your own Web site.

This tutorial teaches you everything about HTML.

HTML is easy to learn - You will enjoy it.

Write HTML Using Notepad or Text Edit

HTML can be edited by using professional HTML editors like:

- Microsoft Web Matrix
- Sublime Text

However, for learning HTML we recommend a text editor like Notepad (PC) or Text Edit (Mac).

We believe using a simple text editor is a good way to learn HTML.

Follow the 4 steps below to create your first web page with Notepad.

Step 1: Open Notepad

To open Notepad in Windows

Click **Start** (bottom left on your screen). Click **All Programs**. Click **Accessories**. Click **Notepad**.

To open Notepad in Windows 8 or later:

Open the **Start Screen** (the window symbol at the bottom left on your screen). Type **Notepad**.

HTML
CSS
5
3

HTM DOCUMENTS

The HTML document itself begins with **<html>** and ends with **</html>**.

The visible part of the HTML document is between **<body>** and **</body>**.

```
<!DOCTYPE html>
<html>
<body>

<h1>My First Heading</h1>

<p>My first paragraph.</p>

</body>
</html>
```

index.htm
file:///C:/Users/myuser/Desktop/index.htm
My First Heading
My first paragraph.

HTML Headings

HTML headings are defined with the **<h1>** to **<h6>** tags

```
<h1>This is a heading</h1>
<h2>This is a heading</h2>
<h3>This is a heading</h3>
```

HTML Paragraphs

HTML paragraphs are defined with the **<p>** tag

```
<p>This is a paragraph.</p>
<p>This is another paragraph.</p>
```

HTML Links

HTML links are defined with the **<a>** tag

```
<a href="http://www.w3schools.com">This is a
link</a>
```

8 HTML Images

HTML images are defined with the **<img>** tag.

The source file (**src**), alternative text (**alt**), and size (**width** and **height**) are provided as **attributes**:

```
<img src="w3schools.jpg" alt="W3Schools.com"
width="104" height="142">
```

JPG Images

GIF Images

PNG Images

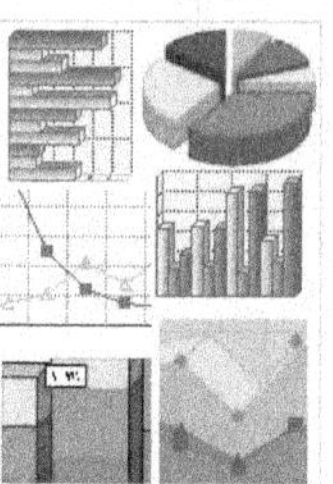

HTML Formatting Elements

HTML also defines special **elements** for defining text with a special **meaning**.

HTML uses elements like <b> and <i> for formatting output, like **bold** or *italic* text.

Formatting elements were designed to display special **types of text**:

HTML TEXT STYLE

HTML Bold

The HTML <b> element defines **bold** text,

```
<b>This text is bold</b>
```

Strong Formatting

```
<strong>This text is strong</strong>
```

HTML *Italic* and *Emphasized* Formatting

The HTML **<i>** element defines *italic* text, without any extra importance.

```
<i>This text is italic</i>
```

The HTML **<em>** element defines *emphasized* text, with added semantic importance.

```
<em>This text is emphasized</em>
```

HTML Small Formatting

The HTML **<small>** element defines **small** text:

```
<small>This text is emphasized</small>
```

HTML Images tag.Syntax

In HTML, images are defined with the **<img>**

```
<img src="html5.jpg" alt="HTML Icon" width="128" height="128">
```

Defining HTML Tables

Example explained:

Tables are defined with the **<table>** tag.

Tables are divided into **table rows** with the **<tr>** tag.

Table rows are divided into **table data** with the **<td>** tag.

A table row can also be divided into **table headings** with the **<th>** tag.

```
<!DOCTYPE html>

<html>

<head>

<style>

table {

    width:100%;

}
```

```css
table, th, td {

    border: 1px solid black;

    border-collapse: collapse;

}

th, td {

    padding: 5px;

    text-align: left;

}

table#t01 tr:nth-child(even) {

    background-color: #eee;

}

table#t01 tr:nth-child(odd) {

  background-color:#fff;

}

table#t01 th        {

    background-color: black;

    color: white;

}
```

</style>

</head>

```html
<body>

<table>

  <tr>

    <th>First Name</th>

    <th>Last Name</th>

    <th>Points</th>

  </tr>

  <tr>

    <td>Jill</td>

    <td>Smith</td>

    <td>50</td>

  </tr>

  <tr>

    <td>Eve</td>

    <td>Jackson</td>

    <td>94</td>

  </tr>

  <tr>

    <td>John</td>
```

```
    <td>Doe</td>

    <td>80</td>

  </tr>

</table>


<br>


<table id="t01">

  <tr>

    <th>First Name</th>

    <th>Last Name</th>

    <th>Points</th>

  </tr>

  <tr>

    <td>Jill</td>

    <td>Smith</td>

    <td>50</td>

  </tr>

  <tr>

    <td>Eve</td>
```

```html
    <td>Jackson</td>

    <td>94</td>

  </tr>   <tr>

  <td>John</td>

    <td>Doe</td>

    <td>80</td>

  </tr>

</table>

</body>

</html>
```

HTML Table Example

Number	First Name	Last Name	Points
1	Eve	Jackson	94
2	John	Doe	80
3	Adam	Johnson	67
4	Jill	Smith	50

HTML Table Example

Number	First Name	Last Name	Points
1	Eve	Jackson	94
2	John	Doe	80

HTML Layouts

```html
<!DOCTYPE html>

<html>

<head>

<style>

#header {

    background-color:black;

    color:white;

    text-align:center;

    padding:5px;

}

#nav {

    line-height:30px;

    background-color:#eeeeee;

    height:300px;

    width:100px;

    float:left;

    padding:5px;
```

```
}

#section {

    width:350px;

    float:left;

    padding:10px;

}

#footer {

    background-color:black;

    color:white;

    clear:both;

    text-align:center;

    padding:5px;

}

</style>

</head>

<body>


<div id="header">

<h1>City Gallery</h1>

</div>
```

```
<div id="nav">

London<br>

Paris<br>

Tokyo

</div>


<div id="section">

<h2>London</h2>

<p>London is the capital city of England. It is the
most populous city in the United Kingdom,

with a metropolitan area of over 13 million
inhabitants.</p>

<p>Standing on the River Thames, London has been a
major settlement for two millennia,

its history going back to its founding by the Romans,
who named it Londinium.</p>

</div>

<div id="footer">

</div>

</body>

</html>
```

HTML Form

HTML forms contain **form elements**.

Form elements are different types of input elements, checkboxes, radio buttons, submit buttons, and more.

```
<form>
  First name:<br>
  <input type="text" name="firstname"><br>
  Last name:<br>
  <input type="text" name="lastname">
</form>
```

First Name

Last Name

State

Australia

Try it yourself »

Radio Button Input

Radio buttons let a user select ONE of a limited number of choices:

```
<form>
  <input type="radio" name="gender" value="male" checked> Male<br>
  <input type="radio" name="gender" value="female"> Female<br>
  <input type="radio" name="gender" value="other"> Other
</form>
```

HTML Button

```
<button>Submit</button>
```

The HTML <video> Element

To show a video in HTML, use the **<video>** element:

```
<video width="320" height="240" controls>
  <source src="movie.mp4" type="video/mp4">
  <source src="movie.ogg" type="video/ogg">
Your browser does not support the video tag.
</video>
```

```
<!DOCTYPE html>

<html>

<body>


<!-- This is a comment -->

<p>This is a paragraph.</p>

<!-- Comments are not displayed in the browser -->
```

HTML Audio - How It Works

The **controls** attribute adds audio controls, like play, pause, and volume.

```
<audio controls>
  <source src="horse.ogg" type="audio/ogg">
  <source src="horse.mp3" type="audio/mpeg">
Your browser does not support the audio element.
</audio>
```

HTML Colors

TVs and computer screens display colors by combining Red, Green, and Blue light.

Color Names

With CSS, colors can be set by using color names:

Example

Color	**Name**
	Red
	Orange
	Yellow
	Cyan
	Blue

RGB (Red, Green, Blue)

With HTML, RGB color values can be specified using this formula: rgb(red, green, blue)

Each parameter (red, green, and blue) defines the intensity of the color between 0 and 255.

For example, rgb(255,0,0) is displayed as red, because red is set to its highest value (255) and the others are set to 0. Experiment by mixing the RGB values below:

Red	**Green**	**Blue**
255	0	0

rgb(255, 0, 0)

Example

Color	**RGB**
	rgb(255,0,0)
	rgb(255,255,0)

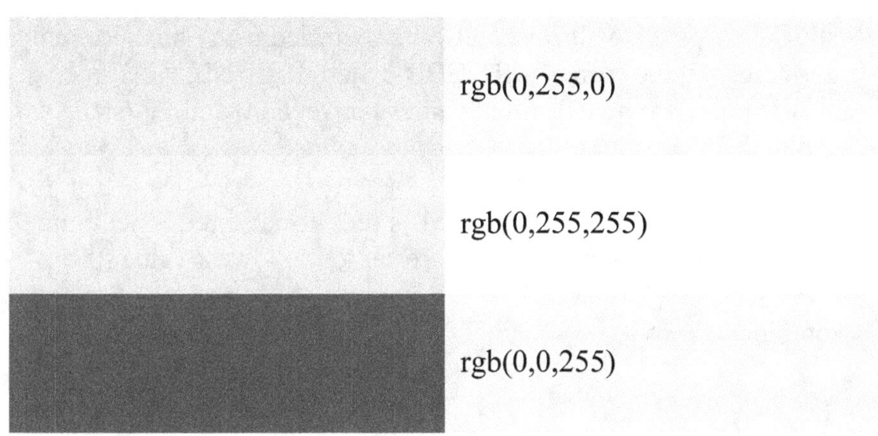

rgb(0,255,0)

rgb(0,255,255)

rgb(0,0,255)

Shades of gray are often defined using equal values for all the 3 light sources:

Example

Color   **RGB**

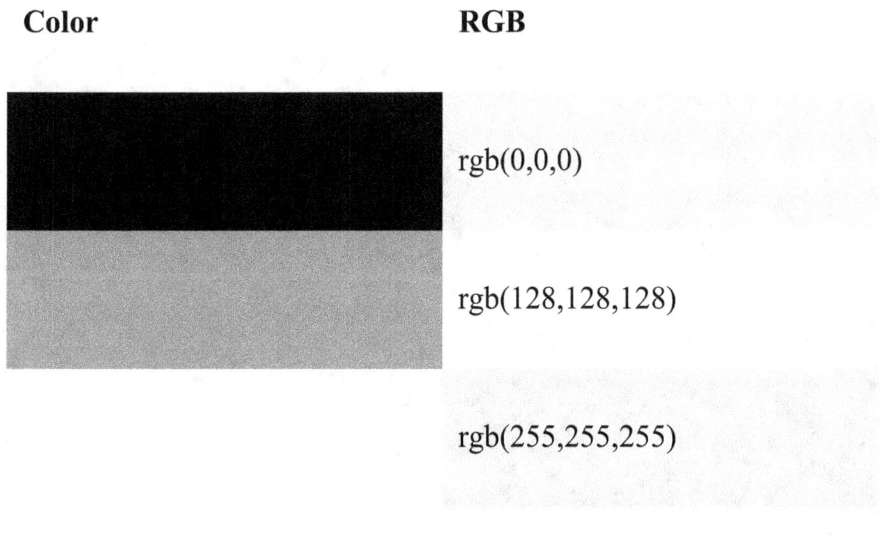

rgb(0,0,0)

rgb(128,128,128)

rgb(255,255,255)

Hexadecimal Colors

With HTML, RGB values can also be specified using hexadecimal color values in the form: #RRGGBB, where RR (red), GG (green) and BB (blue) are hexadecimal values between 00 and FF (same as decimal 0-255).

For example, #FF0000 is displayed as red, because red is set to its highest value (FF) and the others are set to the lowest value (00).

Example

Color	**HEX**
	#FF0000
	#FFFF00
	#00FF00
	#00FFFF
	#0000FF

Shades of gray are often defined using equal values for all the 3 light sources:

Example

Color	HEX
	#000000
	#808080
	#FFFFFF

ABOUT

Mission statement

We enable greatness in people and organization everywhere.

VALUE

Commitment to principles: We are passionate about our content and strive to be models of the principles and practices we teach.